ALLYN & BACON
VideoWorkshop
A COURSE TAILORED VIDEO LEARNING SYSTEM

Introductory Special Education and Inclusion Student Learning Guide with CD-ROM

Second Edition

Diana Murphy
DM Media

PEARSON

Boston   New York   San Francisco
Mexico City   Montreal   Toronto   London   Madrid   Munich   Paris
Hong Kong   Singapore   Tokyo   Cape Town   Sydney

Copyright © 2005 Pearson Education, Inc.

All rights reserved. No part of the material protected by this copyright notice may be reproduced or utilized in any form or by any means, electronic or mechanical, including photocopying, recording, or by any information storage and retrieval system, without written permission from the copyright owner.

To obtain permission(s) to use the material from this work, please submit a written request to Allyn and Bacon, Permissions Department, 501 Boylston Street, Suite 900, Boston, MA 02116 or fax your request to 617-671-2290.

Allyn & Bacon
is an imprint of

PEARSON

www.pearsonhighered.com

ISBN-10: 0-205-45648-0
ISBN-13: 978-0-205-45648-2

Printed in the United States of America

10 9 8   V036   12 11 10

> **This work is protected by United States copyright laws and is provided solely for the use of instructors in teaching their courses and assessing student learning. Dissemination or sale of any part of this work (including on the World Wide Web) will destroy the integrity of the work and is not permitted. The work and materials from it should never be made available to students except by instructors using the accompanying text in their classes. All recipients of this work are expected to abide by these restrictions and to honor the intended pedagogical purposes and the needs of other instructors who rely on these materials.**

Table of Contents

Preface

Module 1: The Profession...1
Video Clip 1: Interview with an Intervention Specialist (3:49)

Module 2: Inclusion and the Least Restrictive Environment...........................4
Video Clip 2: The Inclusive Classroom (8:24)
Video Clip 3: Inclusion of Students with Hearing Impairments (1:56)
Video Clip 4: Assessment of Special Needs Students (2:49)

Module 3: Professional Collaboration..11
Video Clip 5: The Collaborative Process (3:02)
Video Clip 6: Classroom Aides (2:08)

Module 4: Working with Parents and Families..16
Video Clip 7: Working with Parents and Families (3:49)

Module 5: Early Intervention and Early Childhood Special Education........19
Video Clip 8: Early Intervention (4:27)
Video Clip 9: Inclusion in an Early Childhood Class (3:08)

Module 6: Cultural and Linguistic Diversity..24
Video Clip 10: Teaching Bilingual Students (2:41)

Module 7: Learning Disabilities and Attention Deficit Hyperactivity Disorder.................27
Video Clip 11: ADHD (3:33)
Video Clip 12: Learning Disabilities (6:21)

Module 8: Mental Retardation..33
Video Clip 13: Mental Retardation (5:08)

Module 9: Visual and Hearing Impairments...37
Video Clip 14: Visual Impairment (4:34)
Video Clip 15: Hearing Impairment (1:51)

Module 10: Emotional and Behavioral Disorders..43
Video Clip 16: Behavior Disorder (4:22)

Module 11: Traumatic Brain Injury and Physical Disabilities.......................51
Video Clip 17: Traumatic Brain Injury (3:54)
Video Clip 18: Physical Disabilities (3:05)

Module 12: Gifted and Talented..54
Video Clip 19: Challenging Gifted Students (6:16)

Practice Test..59

Preface

This Student Learning Guide accompanies the *Allyn & Bacon VideoWorkshop for Special Education and Inclusion*. It is designed to enhance your experience with the videos.

Features:

- **Learning Objectives** help you focus your learning.
- **Observation Questions** focus on the video itself.
- **Next Step** asks you to go beyond the video by answering questions or completing projects.

Use this grid to correlate the modules in *VideoWorkshop for Special Education and Inclusion* to your Allyn & Bacon textbook.

	Hardman, Drew and Egan *Human Exceptionality*, 8/e	Hallahan and Kauffman *Exceptional Learners*, 9/e	Vaughn, Bos, and Schumm *Teaching Exceptional, Diverse and At-Risk Students*, 3/e	Friend and Bursuck *Including Students with Special Needs*, 3/e	Smith *Introduction to Special Education*, 5/e	Smith et.al – *Teaching Students with Special Needs*, 4e
The Profession	Ch. 2, 3, 4	Ch. 1	Throughout	Ch. 2	Ch. 1	Ch. 15, 16
Inclusion and the Least Restrictive Environment	Ch. 2, 3, 4 and throughout	throughout	Ch. 1	Ch. 1	Ch. 2, throughout	Ch. 1
Professional Collaboration	Ch. 3	throughout	Ch. 4	Ch. 3	Throughout	Ch. 2, 3
Working with Parents and Families	Ch. 3 and Throughout	Throughout	Ch. 4	Ch. 3	Ch. 2	Ch. 3
Early Intervention and Early Childhood	Ch. 3	Ch. 2	Ch. 11	Ch. 1	Throughout	Ch. 4
Cultural and Linguistic Diversity	Ch. 5	Ch. 3	Ch. 10	Ch. 7	Ch. 3	
Learning Disabilities and ADHD	Ch. 7, 8	Ch. 5, 6	Ch. 5	Ch. 6	Ch. 4	Ch. 5, 6
Mental Retardation	Ch. 10	Ch. 4	Ch. 8	Ch. 5	Ch. 6	Ch. 8
Visual and Hearing Impairments	Ch. 15, 16	Ch. 9, 10	Ch. 9	Ch. 5	Ch. 10, 11	Ch. 9
Emotional and Behavioral Disorders	Ch. 9	Ch. 7	Ch. 7	Ch. 6	Ch. 8	Ch. 7
TBI and Physical Disabilities	Ch. 14, 17	Ch. 11, 12	Ch. 9	Ch. 5	Ch. 9	Ch. 10
Gifted and Talented	Ch. 18	Ch. 13	Ch. 12	Ch. 7	Ch. 7	Ch. 12

Student Learning Guide

Module 1: The Profession

Learning Objectives:

After completing this module, you will be able to discuss the role of an intervention specialist and some of the characteristics recommended for the position.

Video Clip 1: Interview with and Intervention Specialist

Observation Questions:

1. What does Lavonne like about working with special needs students?

2. What are the skills Lavonne believes are necessary to be an effective intervention specialist?

Next Step:

1. The National Clearinghouse for Professions in Special Education has a website that includes information on choosing a career in this field. Go to http://www.special-ed-careers.org/, and click on Career Choices in Special Education. Read the articles under "Is special education the career for me?" and answer the following questions:

   - What special education careers sound the most interesting to you? Why?
   - How do salaries for special education teachers compare to general education teachers?
   - Based on what you learn here, do you think you may have an interest in becoming a special education teacher? Explain your answer.

Student Learning Guide

VideoWorkshop for Introductory Special Education and Inclusion

Module 2: Inclusion and the Least Restrictive Environment

Learning Objectives:

After completing this module, you will be able to
1. Discuss the challenges of including students with special needs in the regular education classroom.
2. Describe various accommodations that can be made for students with special needs.

Video Clip 2: The Inclusive Classroom

Observation Questions:

1. How does Penny insure that the students with special needs get the help they need without overlooking the other students in the class?

It appears that Penny has grouped the students with both gen. ed students & sp. ed students at each table. She walks around the room & stops to observe & comment at each table. She makes suggestions to many of the students without singling any one out. As an observer, it's difficult to tell who's who — the students are also expected to support & make suggestions to each other. They must all be in agreement before an answer is recorded.

2. In what ways do the teachers demonstrate cooperative teaching? What are the benefits of working together, as opposed to Penny working with her students in a separate group?

The teachers communicate & interact in front of the students. They model a cooperative model for the children. They respect each other & plan ahead. If Penny were to work alone w/ her students, they would miss out on the whole underlying cooperation lesson going on here. The students may not be able to support & make suggestions to each other.

Next Step:

1. Most students with learning disabilities currently receive their instruction in general education classrooms. Some fear that students who are fully included in the regular education classroom will not get the academic support they need. What would you say to a parent who voiced this concern? When and how should remediation occur when a student is lacking specific prerequisite academic skills, such as writing in complete sentences?

I would try to assure a parent that their child is being observed & evaluated on a regular/ongoing basis. If the teacher sees the child struggling in any way, additional support may be given in the reg classroom either on an individual basis or in their group. It never hurts to review the information with the other students. As we saw in this clip - several of the students forgot to write in complete sentences.

2. What kinds of accommodations might be made for a student with learning disabilities in the regular education classroom? How would you make these accommodations without negatively impacting the other students in the class?

Depending on the disability and the need, accomodations can be made for almost any student in the reg. classroom. I would try to set my classroom up like a community where everyone has a "job" (based on their own skills). Every job is important & vital to the success of the community. Some reg. ed. students could be mentors in various skills & work with the sped. students. It's important for all students to see that everyone brings something to the community.

Student Learning Guide

Video Clip 3: Inclusion of Students with Hearing Impairments

1. What accommodations are made for the student with the hearing impairment?

Next Step:

2. Students who rely on sign language for communication are often isolated from their peers because of difficulties with communication. Some feel that these students should be placed in a separate program with other deaf students who use the same form of communication. What do you think? How does this fit with the concept of least restrictive environment?

3. Having a full time sign language interpreter in the classroom for one student is an expensive proposition for a school district. What other kinds of accommodations could be made in the classroom for a hearing impaired student?

Video Clip 4: Assessment of Special Needs Students

Observation Question:

1. Name six types of accommodations that can be made when testing children with special needs.

   ① Presentation mode - admin. idiv., examiner reads aloud, computer-admin. form, large print, Braille, directions are signed, trusted examiner

   ② Location - reduced distractions, special furniture, spec. lighting

   ③ Response mode - help mark responses, spec. lined paper, comm. device, time limits extended

   ④ Test content - # of items per pg reduced, bilingual glossary

   ⑤ Test format - items are magnified

   ⑥ Authentic assessment - students allowed to show "hands-on" their mastery of info.

2. At the beginning of the clip, the expert mentions the need to use authentic assessment. What is this, and why is it useful with students with special needs?

   Authentic assessment requires students to construct, perform, produce or demonstrate a task or knowledge. This type of assessment is very useful for sp.ed (+ all students) because it is capable of testing their knowledge of a subject & NOT their ability to read & write. Standardized tests require reading + often writing skills. With Auth. Assess Sp. Ed. students are able to demonstrate what they do know and feel good about their knowledge.

Next Step:

3. Schools are being held more accountable for student progress, which is typically assessed with standardized tests. Many students with special needs are unable to be assessed this way. Schools are still accountable, however, for the progress of these students. What alternate kinds of assessments might be used, and how can a teacher insure that the right skills are being measured?

Alternate kinds of assessment include:
1) Informal Tests - more loosely structured - used to monitor day-to-day growth in learning.
(CRT) 2) Criterion-referenced testing - compares a students performance w/ a criterion of mastery for a specific skill - regardless of group standing.
3) Authentic Assessment - requires students to perform, produce, construct or demonstrate knowledge
4) Portfolio Assessment - a collection of assessments over time to show progress
5) Ecological Assessment - how well one operates in their environment
*focus shift from one's deficits toward how to build strengths

(*) A probe is a simple test created by the teacher to measure a specific task has been learned. Often used to review a child's 'response to intervention'.

Student Learning Guide

Module 3: Professional Collaboration

Learning Objectives:

After completing this module, you will be able to
1. Explain what cooperative teaching is, and how it benefits students.
2. Describe the benefits to students and teachers of using classroom aides.

Video Clip 5: The Collaborative Process

Observation Question:

1. In what ways do the students in this video benefit from having these two teachers plan the lesson together?

Collaboration - support the needs of each other - teachers work together & can attend to the needs of every child, from home to classroom. When the lesson is planned by both teachers, gen ed. & sp. ed. children are a part of the classroom lesson so they can be included - They also have the opportunity to learn from their peers - Both groups benefit from each other -

Next Step:

2. As a new teacher, how comfortable do you think you would be with having another teacher in your classroom helping teach a subject? What are some ways you could work with the teacher, or collaborate, to make the experience more beneficial to both you and your students?

I think I would welcome the chance to have another teacher in the room. This is a great opportunity to join ideas, problem solve together & collaborate lessons. It's also another pair of eyes, ears & hands. Sounds like a win-win to me. I would work together by one teach/one observe, team teach, alternative teaching, parallel teach, station teach & one teach/one drift.

3. Why is collaboration important to the process of inclusion?

Collaboration is very impt. for the gen. ed. & sp. ed. teachers of a sp. ed. student because it's very important to keep the learning moving forward in a positive way. If both teachers are doing their own thing - students may feel confused and overwhelmed, especially if the 2 lessons ever contradict each other. It's best to work together for the good of the student.

4. Take a minute and think about all the teams you have been involved with.
   - Which of these teams worked well?
   - Which were not successful in meeting their goals?
   - What characteristics of collaboration were present in the teams that were successful?
   - What characteristics of collaboration were NOT present in the teams that were unsuccessful?

The teams that work the best are probably the ones that are able to communicat the best. When everyone is on a different page, its difficult for the team to "win". Winning teams communicate, learn to give & take, compromise, wants what's good for the team, are honest & forthright.

5. The speech/language therapist comes once a week to work with Suzanne in your classroom. Today she spent half-an-hour working on new vocabulary words with Suzanne. When she finished her work, she wanted to speak with your immediately, even though you were working with a reading group. She was very insistent and would not agree to speak later on the phone. How would you handle this situation and remain collaborative with this professional?

I would ask her to wait a few minutes until I was finished with my group. If she couldn't, I think I would quickly try to get the group to a point where they were working independently & then listen to the therapist. Later, I might bring the situation up & discuss my concern w/ the interuption. A good team needs to give & take. This time I might need to give & next time she might need to give.

VideoWorkshop for Introductory Special Education and Inclusion

Video Clip 6: Classroom Aides

Observation Questions:

1. What was the role of the aide in this classroom? What do you think the outcome would be if this student didn't have an aide?

Next Step:

2. How does the use of an aide in the classroom help the school meet the provisions of IDEA? Check your textbook for information about IDEA, or go to http://www.ed.gov/offices/OSERS/Policy/IDEA/index.html for a copy of the Act.

3. You are a third grade teacher, it is a week before school starts, and you've just been informed that you will have a student in your class with a full-time aide. What questions would you want answered? How would you prepare for having this extra person in your classroom?

Module 4: Working with Parents and Families

Learning Objectives:

After completing this module, you will be able to
1. Explain various ways to involve parents in the educational process.

Video Clip 7: Working with Parents and Families

Observation Question:

1. Why should parents be actively involved in their child's education?

2. Why might some teachers be apprehensive about having parents in the classroom? What else can a teacher do to involve parents?

___

Next Step:

3. Interview the parent of a child with a disability. Ask the parent to fill out a log for one week prior to the interview that indicates all the activities in which he or she participated with the child.
    - Was this parent actively involved in the educational process? In what ways?
    - If not, why not?
    - What conclusions can you draw from this activity?

4. Often educators fail to understand the effects that a sibling with disabilities can have on the other children in the family and therefore affect family life. Visit the following websites and identify and list the issues faced by siblings or ways that siblings respond to the person with a disability. What is your response to these issues? How can educators help families deal with these issues?

http://www.familyvillage.wisc.edu/general/frc_sibl.htm
http://www.nas.com/downsyn/siblings.html

5. As a special educator, if you feel that the least restrictive environment (LRE) for a particular student is not the general education classroom, how might you go about working with a parent who is strongly in favor of inclusion only?

Module 5: Early Intervention and Early Childhood Special Education

Learning Objectives:

After completing this module, you will be able to
1. Explain the benefits of early intervention for children with special needs.
2. Describe the ways that preschool is beneficial to children with special needs

Video Clip 8: Early Intervention

Observation Questions:

1. What are the benefits of preschool for children with special needs?

2. Why is early intervention important with children at risk?

Next Step:

3. What does federal law require in terms of early intervention for children with disabilities? Find out if your state has other requirements, and list them here.

2. What is the role of the parent in the early intervention process? How can preschool teachers get parents more involved in their child's classroom?

VideoWorkshop for Introductory Special Education and Inclusion

Video Clip 9: Inclusion in Early Childhood Education

Observation Question:

1. What are the benefits of inclusion in preschool for a child with special needs, and for that child's peers?

___

Next Step:

2. Many states have a special education category called "developmentally delayed" that can be used to identify students needing special education services up to age 9. Why would states have such a category, and how can it be useful for early childhood teachers?

_____

_____

_____

_____

_____

_____

3. As a student with special needs progresses from the early childhood classroom through the grade levels, how might the benefits and limitations of inclusion change for the student?

_____

_____

_____

_____

_____

_____

_____

Module 6: Cultural and Language Diversity

Learning Objectives:

After completing this module, you will be able to
1. Discuss the challenges of teaching in a bilingual classroom
2. Describe the arguments in support of and opposed to bilingual instruction in this country.

Video Clip 10: Teaching Bilingual Students

Observation Question:

1. In what way is teaching children from diverse cultures a special challenge?

Student Learning Guide

2. What techniques are demonstrated by the teachers in this clip to facilitate instruction?

___

Next Step:

3. The debate over the efficacy of bilingual instruction has gone on for years and will most likely continue in this country. Browse the Internet for articles on both sides of this subject, and write about your views in a paper.

___

4. You are a middle school teacher with four different language groups represented in your classroom, and you know only half a dozen words in each of the languages. The school's resources are very limited. Pick one topic and tell how you would teach it to accommodate the limited English proficiency of your students.

Module 7: Learning Disabilities and Attention Deficit Hyperactivity Disorder

Learning Objectives:

After completing this module, you will be able to
1. List the characteristics of ADHD, and discuss the currently available treatments.
2. Discuss the educational implications for a child with ADHD.
3. Define the most common learning disabilities, and discuss the educational implications for each.
4.

Video Clip 11: ADHD

Observation Question:

1. What characteristics of ADHD does Eric demonstrate?

2. Based on what you have learned about Eric, do you believe he should be included in a regular education classroom? Explain.

___

Next Step:

3. What biological causes have been determined for ADHD?

___

4. Many people oppose the use of drugs like Ritalin to control the behaviors associated with ADHD. Others feel they are simply prescribed too frequently, and before other measures have been taken to deal with the problem.
    - Browse the Internet for issues and information from both sides of the discussion. Summarize your findings.
    - What is your opinion on the use of prescription medications with young children? With adults?

_____

_____

_____

_____

_____

_____

_____

_____

1. Eric's educational planning was complicated by the fact that he had some emotional issues in addition to ADHD. As his teacher, what resources would you draw upon to insure that all of Eric's needs were being met?

_____

_____

_____

_____

_____

_____

_____

_____

VideoWorkshop for Introductory Special Education and Inclusion

Video Clip 12: Learning Disabilities

Observation Question:

1. What symptoms of dyslexia does Bridget exhibit? What concerns does she have about the effect dyslexia will have on her future?

Bridget has a hard time reading & spelling so as a result, she does not like to read & spell. She has a hard time comprehending - this even applies to class exams. Her difficulty with spelling impacts her ability to write as well. She & Her mom are worried about college - even though she plans to go. Will there be help for Bridget if she needs it? She's also concerned about holding a job - should she tell them about her disability? Also will she mess up & "ruin the business".

Next Step:

2. Choose a common learning disability and write a brief summary of the topic. You may use your textbook or one of the following websites as a starting point.

   International Dyslexia Association - http://www.interdys.org/index.jsp
   Council for Learning Disabilities - http://www.cldinternational.org
   Learning Disabilities Association - http://www.ldanatl.org/

Student Learning Guide

_____

_____

_____

_____

3. Go to this link on the PBS special about children with learning disabilities:
   http://www.pbs.org/wgbh/misunderstoodminds/

   - On the left side of the main frame you will find links to Attention, Reading, Writing, and Mathematics. Follow these links to simulation activities.
   - Click on at least one of these on each page.
   - Discuss what you learned from trying the simulation.

_____

_____

_____

_____

_____

_____

_____

4. Many students with learning disabilities have difficulty making and maintaining friendships.
   - What characteristics of learning disabilities contribute to this problem? low self esteem, others don't understand different, resource room
   - How do each of the characteristics you named cause problems with interpersonal relationships? with draw, ashamed, left out
   - Bridget experienced success in her general education classes. What characteristics of Bridget's contributed to this success? What characteristics of a student with a learning disability might make a resource room a more appropriate setting for part of the school day?

Bridget was outgoing, attractive (didn't look like she had a disability), motivated, desire to do well & 'fit in', able to advocate for herself and ask for help when she needed it (like taking exams). Others who are not so motivated may benefit more from the 1-1 help, those who don't advocate for themselves will need a teacher who understands their needs, someone to work more closely with them to keep them organized. Also may be a student who doesn't have a lot of support from home.

Student Learning Guide

Module 8: Mental Retardation

Learning Objectives:

After completing this module, you will be able to
1. List the characteristics of the different levels of mental retardation.
2. Discuss the educational implications for a child with mental retardation.

Video Clip 13: Mental Retardation

Observation Question:

1. On which skills did the pre-school teacher focus with Carlyn?

[Handwritten notes in margin: role models, expectations, walking, "talk + sounds", feeding, academically, fine motor shapes, categorize, puzzle, peer learning]

33

VideoWorkshop for Introductory Special Education and Inclusion

2. What does Carlyn gain by being included with higher functioning children?

_____

_____

_____

_____

_____

_____

_____

Next Step:

3. Based on what you know from this video, in which adaptive skills is Carlyn likely to have deficits in the future?

_____

_____

_____

_____

_____

_____

_____

Student Learning Guide

4. What is the definition of moderate, severe and profound mental retardation? From what you could see of Carlyn's learner characteristics and physical needs, at what level do you believe Carlyn is functioning?

_____

_____

_____

_____

_____

_____

_____

5. The topic of inclusion of students with mental retardation is often a controversial one.
    - Select a partner from your class to brainstorm the benefits and challenges of teaching a class that includes a student with MR.
    - Be sure to discuss all factors, not just the disability, including the student's behavior, family support, reactions of other students and their families, and special education support services.
    - Once you have generated a list, write a personal reflection discussing your position regarding inclusion of students with MR in general education classrooms.

_____

_____

_____

_____

_____

_____

Module 9: Visual and Hearing Impairments

Learning Objectives:

After completing this module, you will be able to
1. Explain how a visual impairment impacts a child's educational progress.
2. Discuss accommodations teachers can make for a child with a visual impairment.
3. Explain how a hearing impairment impacts a child's educational progress.
4. Discuss accommodations teachers can make for a child with a hearing impairment.

Video Clip 14: Visual Impairment

Observation Questions:

1. What are some ways that Kyle compensates for his visual impairment?

2. What special accommodations do his family and teacher make to enable him to function both in and out of school?

Next Step:

3. What kinds of learning difficulties would you expect from someone with a visual impairment? What accommodations might a regular classroom teacher make to enable this student to succeed in the classroom? You will find resources to help you answer this question at http://www.glc.k12.ga.us/trc/search.asp?mode=result&intpathid=209&strKeyword=Visual+Impairment.

4. What kinds of equipment are available for visually impaired students, and how would these devices help in the classroom? You may want begin with a visit the website for the American Printing House for the Blind - http://www.aph.org/.

5. Teaching activities of daily living and orientation and mobility skills are content areas that are especially important for students with visual impairments.
   - Explain why these are important.
   - Explain why social skills will be one of the necessary activities of daily living.
   - How can these content areas be integrated into the routine teaching activities in your classroom?

VideoWorkshop for Introductory Special Education and Inclusion

Video Clip 15: Hearing Impairment

Observation Questions:

1. What special accommodations does this student require in the classroom?

2. The aide refers to the need for the teacher to use more visual teaching techniques. What kinds of things might she be referring to?

Next Step:

3. Experience what it is like to have a hearing loss by wearing earplugs to class one day and sitting in the back of the room. What does your instructor do that hinders your understanding of the content taught? What is done to aid comprehension? How might your instructor modify his or her teaching to accommodate having a hearing-impaired student in the class? Check to see what your school offers in the way of help for students with hearing deficits: sign language interpreters, closed caption video, amplifiers, etc.

4. The student in this video has partial hearing and her speech is understandable. Search the Internet for articles on the oral approach versus sign language. What do you think is the best method of communication for a child, and why? Another topic you may explore is the difference of opinion about the use of cochlear implants.

5. Discuss the instructional implications of teaching content, beyond reading and language arts, and classroom management for general education teachers who are teaching students who are deaf or hard of hearing. Suggest an accommodation, adaptation or modification that would help meet each of these implications.

6. Placing students who are deaf in general education classrooms for all of their school day remains controversial. Parents are often unsure which professionals have the right answers. Consider both sides of this issue, then outline a plan for helping teachers and parents sort through the issues so that they may make an appropriate decision for each student.

Student Learning Guide

Module 10: Emotional and Behavioral Impairments

Learning Objectives:

After completing this module, you will be able to
1. Explain how emotional and behavioral impairments impact a child's educational progress.
2. Discuss accommodations teachers can make for a child with emotional or behavioral impairments.

Video Clip 16: Behavior Disorder

Observation Questions:

1. What kinds of inappropriate behavior did Nick demonstrate?

Nick does not follow the teachers directions well, he does not take responsibility for his actions / blames others, inappropriate ways of dealing w/ friends - hitting, grabbing things away, getting angry w/ others, push & shove, lack of self-control, not able to self-evaluate (blames others), noncompliant, running in halls, verbal aggression toward teachers.

43

VideoWorkshop for Introductory Special Education and Inclusion

2. How did the special educators at Nick's school address these behaviors?

He was put into a self contained classroom (Behaviorally Handicapped) where he was taught social skills & appropriate behaviors - how to deal w/ others. Later moved to the Strong Program that seemed to fit him better. He was academically able but needed help w/ different behaviors that were not totally unmanageable.

Next Step:

3. What qualifies a person to be designated as behaviorally disordered, as opposed to just being someone who gets in trouble for inappropriate behavior?

4. From what you have learned from your text and classroom discussion, what are some methods of instruction that a teacher in a regular education classroom might use with Nick?

5. Students with behavior disorders can display two types of behavior problems: externalizing or internalizing.
    - Compare and contrast these two behaviors patterns.
    - Identify ways to manage two of these behaviors in the classroom.

VideoWorkshop for Introductory Special Education and Inclusion

Module 11: Traumatic Brain Injury and Physical Disabilities

Learning Objectives:

After completing this module, you will be able to
1. Explain how TBI and physical disabilities impact a child's educational progress.
2. Discuss accommodations teachers can make for a child with TBI or physical disabilities disabilities.

Video Clip 17: Traumatic Brain Injury

Observation Questions:

1. What disabilities does Matt have as a result of the TBI?

_____

_____

_____

_____

_____

_____

_____

_____

2. What skills are his teachers focusing on to enable him to eventually be included in a regular education classroom?

_____

_____

_____

_____

_____

_____

_____

Next Step:

3. Search for the more common causes of TBI by age. Imagine that you are assigned to create an informational poster or brochure on prevention of TBI. Use the space below to brainstorm what information you feel is more relevant to educate parents and the community.

_____

_____

_____

_____

_____

_____

_____

Video Clip 18: Physical Disabilities

Observation Questions:

1. What special adaptations are made for Oscar to be able to participate in the math lesson?

Next Step:

2. Use a wheelchair or any other prosthetic device for at least 3-4 hours while conducting your daily routine.
    - Did you find that your interactions with others were different in any way? What else was different?
    - What did you learn through your simulation of a physical disability?
    - How might this information help you as a teacher of a physically disabled student?

_____
_____
_____
_____
_____
_____
_____
_____

3. Assistive technology is critically important for students with physical disabilities. Select and describe the purpose for a hardware appliance, software program, or adaptation for the following students.
    a. Student with paraplegia
    b. Student with limited use of hands and arms
    c. Student who is nonverbal.

    You will find help for this activity in your text and at thses web sites:
    - Closing the Gap www.closingthegap.com/
    - Alphasmart is an inexpensive, personal word processing device. http://www.alphasmart.com/
    - Encarta offers a talking dictionary. Type in a word into the "Find a word" space and follow the links. http://dictionary.msn.com/
    - Alex Catalog is located at Oxford University. http://www.infomotions.com/alex/
    - Web Copier allows persons to copy websites for off line use. http://www.maximumsoft.com/

2. Explore how the instruction from the teacher would need to differ for Oscar in relation to students without disabilities and how Oscar's presence could contribute to and detract from the class. How much instruction would come from the classroom teacher versus the instructional assistant? Did Oscar appear to be on grade level? If not, what might the other student be working on and how could Oscar be integrated?

Module 12: Gifted and Talented

Learning Objective:

After completing this module, students will be able to
1. Define the term "gifted," and explain how these students are identified.
2. Understand the intellectual skills that are common to gifted students.

Video Clip 19: Challenging Gifted Learners

Observation Questions:

1. List instances from the video clip where students demonstrate the following intellectual skills that are common to gifted students:
    - formulates abstractions
    - processes information in complex ways
    - observant
    - excited about new ideas
    - enjoys hypothesizing
    - learns rapidly
    - uses a large vocabulary
    - inquisitive

Next Step:

2. What does it mean to be "gifted?" How are these students typically identified?

3. There is debate over which is the best way to teach gifted students. What are the advantages and disadvantages of acceleration and enrichment programs? You may find links to information to help you answer this question at http://www.cfw.tufts.edu/viewtopics.asp?categoryid=3&topicid=67.

4. Are all students in AP classes "gifted?" Would students who are not gifted benefit from the instruction provided in this clip? Explain.

VideoWorkshop for Introductory Special Education and Inclusion

Practice Test

Instructions:
Test your recall of the information presented in the video clips by circling the appropriate answer choice for each question below. The clips that correspond to each question are listed for your review.

1. The knowledge that Lavonne Dursch mentioned as being important for an intervention specialist include all of the following except
Video Clip 1

    A. the developmental characteristics of children at different ages
    B. the district curriculum
    C. methods of assessment
    D. academic theory

2. In the video, "Becoming a Teacher," how does Penny Brandenburg involve her students in the learning process?
Video Clip 2

    A. She uses self-assessment as a means of measuring progress.
    B. She focuses on the students' needs, giving them some control over the process.
    C. She uses discipline to maintain order in the classroom.
    D. She lets them choose what they are going to learn.

3. Which of the following examples demonstrates the concept of collaboration?
Video Clip 5

    A. A classroom teacher and special education teacher agree to send a child with reading problems to a resource room for extra help.
    B. A reading specialist comes into the classroom to work with children who need it.
    C. Two fourth grade teachers co-teach a unit on rocks and minerals.
    D. All of the above.

4. The most common barrier to collaboration is _____.
Video Clip 5

   A. district support
   B. time to prepare lesson plans
   C. time to plan and work with their team
   D. extra compensation

5. According to the video clip, "Working with Parents and Families," why should parents be actively involved in their children's education?
Video Clip 7

   A. Parents are the driving force behind their child's education.
   B. Teachers are overworked and need help in the classroom.
   C. Children work harder when their parents are involved.
   D. None of these was mentioned.

6. Bilingualism is defined as
Video Clip 10

   A. speaking a language other than English.
   B. speaking English as a second language.
   C. not speaking English.
   D. having proficiency in two languages.

7. Students who are ESL include those who
Video Clip 10

   A. speak a language other than English.
   B. speak English as a second language.
   C. do not speak English
   D. have proficiency in two languages.

8. ADHD is a condition that affects
Video Clip 11

   A. young children only.
   B. children of any age.
   C. school-age children only.
   D. both children and adults.

9. The most commonly used intervention for ADHD is _____.
Video Clip 11

   A. Cognitive Behavior Management
   B. Positive Reinforcement Schedule
   C. Depressant medications
   D. Psychostimulant medications

10. Severe impairment of the ability to read is a symptom of which learning disability?
Video Clip 12

   A. Dyslexia
   B. ADHD
   C. Dyscalculia
   D. Aphasia

11. Students with learning disabilities have difficulty learning because _____.
Video Clip 12

   A. they have below-average cognitive ability
   B. they live in a socio-economic disadvantaged environment
   C. they have processing deficits
   D. they lack motivation for academic work

12. Severity levels of mental retardation are determined by scores on intelligence tests and limitations in _____ skills.
Video Clip 13

   A. academic
   B. employment
   C. adaptive
   D. self-care

13. Functional curriculum often helps students with moderate to severe cognitive disabilities to develop _____ skills.
Video Clip 13

   A. vocational
   B. real-life
   C. social
   D. academic

14. Adaptive skills characteristics include all of the following EXCEPT _____.
Video Clip 13

   A. taking care of personal skills
   B. developing interpersonal relationships
   C. difficulties learning vocational skills
   D. difficulties coping with environmental demands

15. What is one reason why students who are visually impaired may need to delay their graduation from high school?
Video Clip 14

   A. To learn more content so they can pass the exit exam.
   B. To have more orientation and mobility instruction.
   C. To learn to read more quickly in Braille or large print.
   D. To learn skills required for independent living.

16. A student who is legally blind may not qualify for special education services or have an IEP. How is this possible?
Video Clip 14

   A. The student may be able to use print for learning.
   B. The student's parents would not sign the IEP.
   C. The student reads Braille proficiently.
   D. The student can use hearing for a majority of learning tasks.

17. One reason students with visual impairments struggle with academic work is _____.
Video Clip 14

   A. They have lower cognitive ability than typical learners.
   B. They are unable to focus on the physical environment.
   C. They have fewer opportunities to acquire information.
   D. They have difficulty interacting appropriately with others.

18. Behavior is classified as disordered when _____.
Video Clip 16

   A. it affects personal adjustment
   B. it differs from behavior of peers
   C. it affects employment
   D. all of the above

19. Students with TBI often experience _____.
Video Clip 17

    A. Loss of cognitive capacity
    B. Social and emotional difficulties
    C. Limited use of limbs
    D. Recovery from injuries within a year or two

20. Which of the following is considered traumatic brain injury?
Video Clip 17

    A. a head hits the windshield in a car accident and the victim loses consciousness
    B. a man suffers a stroke and loses his ability to understand speech
    C. a drug overdose leaves its victim in a coma
    D. none of the above

Practice Test Answer Key

1. D
2. B
3. D
4. C
5. A
6. D
7. B
8. D
9. D
10. A
11. C
12. C
13. B
14. C
15. D
16. A
17. C
18. D
19. B
20. A

Notes

Notes